A Note to Parents

DK READERS is a compelling new program for beginning readers, designed in conjunction with leading literacy experts, including Dr. Linda Gambrell, Director of the School of Education at Clemson University. Dr. Gambrell has served on the Board of Directors of the International Reading Association and as President of the National Reading Conference.

Beautiful illustrations and superb full-color photographs combine with engaging, easy-to-read stories to offer a fresh approach to each subject in the series. Each DK READER is guaranteed to capture a child's interest while developing his or her reading skills, general knowledge, and love of reading.

The four levels of DK READERS are aimed at different reading abilities, enabling you to choose the books that are exactly right for your child:

Level 1 – Beginning to read
Level 2 – Beginning to read alone
Level 3 – Reading alone
Level 4 – Proficient readers

The "normal" age at which a child begins to read can be anywhere from three to eight years old, so these levels are intended only as a general guideline.

No matter which level you select, you can be sure that you are helping your child learn to read, then read to learn!

LONDON, NEW YORK, MUNICH,
MELBOURNE, AND DELHI

Editor Sheila Hanly
Art Editor Jill Plank
Senior Editor Linda Esposito
Senior Art Editor
Diane Thistlethwaite
U.S. Editor Regina Kahney
Cover Designer Margherita Gianni
Production Melanie Dowland
Picture Researcher Andrea Sadler
Illustrator Peter Dennis
Natural History Consultant
Theresa Greenaway

Reading Consultant
Linda B. Gambrell, Ph.D.

First American Edition, 1999
05 10 9 8 7 6 5 4
Published in the United States by DK Publishing, Inc.
375 Hudson Street, New York, New York 10014

Published in Great Britain by Dorling Kindersley Limited.

Library of Congress Cataloging-in-Publication Data
Platt, Richard
   Plants bite back! / by Richard Platt. — 1st American ed.
   p.   cm. — (Dorling Kindersley readers. Level 3)
   Summary: Introduces stinging plants, poisonous plants, and plants
   that eat animals.
   ISBN 0-7894-4755-X (hc). — ISBN 0-7894-4754-1 (pbk.)
   1. Poisonous plants Juvenile literature. 2. Dangerous plants
Juvenile literature. 3. Carnivorous plants Juvenile literature.
[1. Poisonous plants. 2. Carnivorous plants. 3. Dangerous plants.]
I. Title. II. Series.
OK100.A1P58 1999
581.6'5—dc21   99-20403
                                              CIP

Color reproduction by Colourscan, Singapore
Printed and bound in China by L Rex Printing Co., Ltd.

The publisher would like to thank the following for their kind permission
to reproduce their photographs:
Key: t=top, a=above, b=below, l=left, r=right, c=center
Heather Angel: 10 l, 13 t, 19 t; **Ardea London Ltd:** John Mason 25 r,
Y. Arthus-Bertrand 44 cl; **Biofotos:** Paul Simons 14 cl; **Bridgeman Art Library,
London / New York:** 40 bc; **Bruce Coleman Ltd:** John Cancalosi 39, Kim Taylor 11,
Leonard Lee Rue 43 tc; **Ronald Grant Archive:** 13 br; **N.H.P.A:** G.I. Bernard 12
crb, George Gainsburgh 12 cra; **Oxford Scientific Films:** Peter Parks 12 cr; Photos
Horticultural: 41 clb; **Planet Earth Pictures:** Frank Krahmer 42 br; **Royal
Horticultural Society:** 33; **Science Photo Library:** David Nunuk 18 tr,
Dr P. Marazzi 24 cl, Sue Ford 47 t
Jacket: Heather Angel: front c, back c; **Image Quest:** Peter Parks front c; **Photos
Horticultural:** Michael and Lois Warren front c; **Science Photo Library:** Claude
Nuridsany/Marie Perennou front c; **Tony Stone Images:** front c.
All other images © Dorling Kindersley.
For further information see www.dkimages.com

Discover more at

www.dk.com

Contents

PLANTS
BITE BACK!

Written by Richard Platt

DK

DK Publishing, Inc.

Plant power

Plants cover the surface of the earth. Without them, we could not survive. One of their most important jobs is to provide food for animals and people.

But not all plants can be munched for lunch. Some make bitter poisons to keep animals from eating them.

There are no flies on this plant – it's eaten them all! See how the **Venus flytrap** *catches insects on pages 6–9.*

NORTH AMERICA

EUROPE

AFRICA

SOUTH AMERICA

Beware of the giant **Saguaro cactus** *on page 38 – it's covered in thousands of sharp spines.*

Find out why this tree is called the **candelabra tree** *on page 42.*

4

Some arm themselves with spikes or stings. Others turn the tables completely – they catch animals and eat THEM!

Every country in the world has its share of stinging, scratching, and biting plants. This map shows where some of them grow – and where you will find them in the pages ahead.

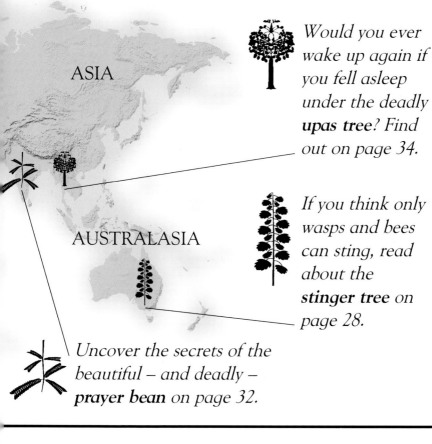

ASIA

Would you ever wake up again if you fell asleep under the deadly **upas tree**? Find out on page 34.

AUSTRALASIA

If you think only wasps and bees can sting, read about the **stinger tree** on page 28.

Uncover the secrets of the beautiful – and deadly – **prayer bean** on page 32.

Greedy green guzzlers

On the edge of a swamp, a damselfly flies over a plant with strange-looking leaves. The damselfly hovers, then lands. SNAP! The comb-shaped sides of the leaf spring together and trap the damselfly.

The plant is a Venus flytrap. It is a carnivorous (car-NIV-er-uss), or meat-eating plant. These plants are unusual.

Of the 250,000 different kinds of plants on earth, only about 400 are carnivorous.

Carnivorous plants grow in marshes or bogs. Boggy soil does not contain enough of the minerals that plants need to grow well. Carnivorous plants get an extra supply of these minerals by eating insects. They can survive without eating insects, but the extra minerals help them to grow better.

The Venus flytrap grows in marshland in North and South Carolina.

Catching insects is not easy when you are a plant. The Venus flytrap has no eyes to see flies. It has no ears to hear the hum of a honeybee. So how does it lure its lunch?

Like every trap, the Venus flytrap contains bait. Sugary nectar covers the leaves. Insects smell the nectar. They think it's mealtime. They are right, but they never guess THEY are on the menu.

Trigger hair

Once the damselfly touches the trigger hairs the leaf closes.

Three tiny hairs on each leaf act as triggers. As soon as an insect touches the hairs, TWANG goes the trap. In less than a second, the sides of the leaf close in over the insect.

After 30 minutes, the trap has shut tightly and filled with liquid. Over a week or two, most of the insect's body dissolves into dead-insect soup. The plant absorbs this liquid food through its leaf surface.

The leaf's spiny edges interlock, so the insect cannot escape.

The Venus flytrap is the only plant with deadly jaws. The bladderwort, another meat-eating plant, has a sneakier way of catching lunch. It sucks up its victims like a vacuum cleaner!

Bladderwort stems and flowers grow above water.

A bladderwort eats tiny water insects and fish. It can swallow fry, or baby fish, in a single bite.

Bladderworts are among the most common of carnivorous plants. They float in ponds. They grow in very wet ground. They even live in puddles of rainwater that form in the cup-shaped leaves of some plants.

This mosquito larva is too big for the bladderwort to swallow – it will probably wiggle free.

You would need a microscope to see a bladderwort catch its prey. On each of its roots are a number of traps that look like tiny bubbles. Each trap has a little door that shuts tight. To set the trap, the plant sucks water out of it. This makes the trap's springy wall cave inward. There are tiny trigger hairs on the trap. If an insect, such as a water flea, touches the hairs, the trap door suddenly opens. The sucked-in sides of the trap spring out. Water rushes in, sucking the flea with it. SNAP!

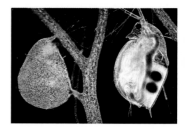

A water flea gets too close to a bladderwort.

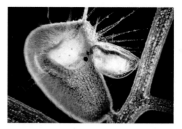

The flea is sucked into the plant's trap.

The bladderwort digests its meal.

A bladderwort's root system, showing the bubble-like traps

The door closes again, trapping the insect inside. This happens in one fiftieth of a second – faster than the eye can see.

But the bladderwort does not bolt its food. A mixture of chemicals in the trap slowly dissolves the water flea's body.

Plants that eat people?
Carnivorous plants mostly eat insects. People-eating plants, such as this one from the movie *Little Shop of Horrors*, exist only in science fiction.

Unlike bladderworts, pitcher plants have no moving parts. Instead, they drown their prey in pools of liquid. These pools are a mixture of water and digestive juices. They form in the plant's leaves, which are shaped like pitchers.

The largest pitcher plants grow in Borneo, an island in Southeast Asia.

These giant pitchers are big enough to trap insects, small birds, frogs, and even rats! The monkey cup pitcher plant gets its name because thirsty monkeys drink from its pitchers. Humans use the pitchers, too – as buckets, and sometimes as cooking pots.

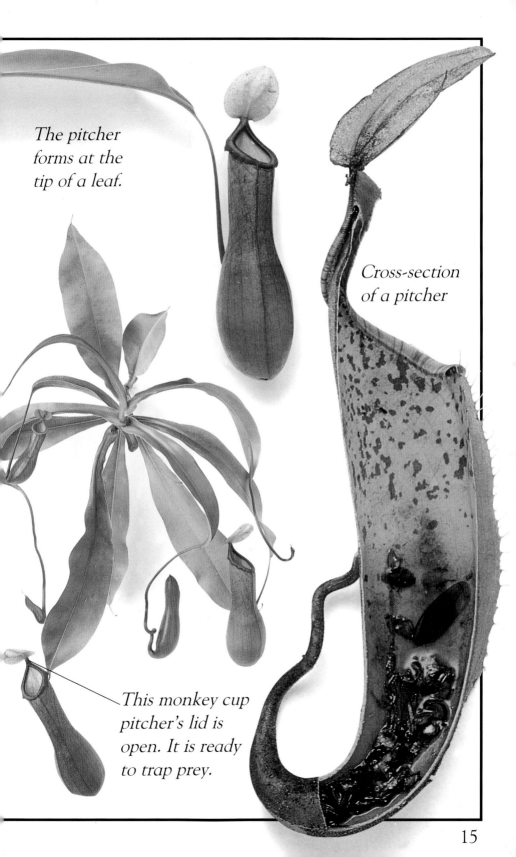

The pitcher forms at the tip of a leaf.

Cross-section of a pitcher

This monkey cup pitcher's lid is open. It is ready to trap prey.

15

But how does a pitcher plant catch its prey? Imagine a fly buzzing through the jungle. It spots a brightly colored pitcher. The fly lands on the pitcher's slippery edge. It smells nectar around the rim. It sees shiny ridges leading down into the pitcher. The hungry fly climbs into the pitcher to suck up the nectar.

But the inner surface of the pitcher is covered in loose, waxy flakes. The fly begins to slip and slide. As it scrabbles and struggles, the waxy flakes peel away and the fly loses its grip. SPLASH! It sinks into the liquid and drowns, and the pitcher plant begins to digest its latest meal.

Glands on the inner surface of the pitcher make digestive juices that dissolve the plant's prey.

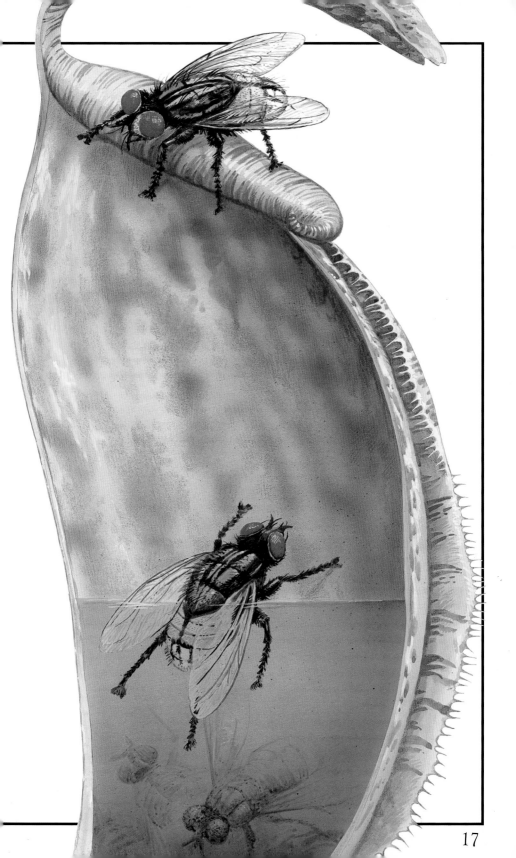

Sundew plants are nature's own flypaper. Their leaves are covered in a shiny goo that lures insects to a sticky end.

The glue-like drops give the plant its name: in sunlight they shine like dew. For unwary insects, the sparkling leaves may be the last thing they see.

A group of sundew plants growing in poor, boggy soil

Although sundews are found all over the world, the greatest variety grows in Australia. The smallest is no bigger than a shirt button. But a few types grow into sticky bushes higher than a grown-up's waist.

Every leaf of the sundew plant is covered in fine hairs. Every hair has a blob of sticky gunk at the tip. When an insect lands on a sundew's leaf, just one touch of one hair is enough to catch and hold the insect.

When the insect tries to get free, it touches another hair … then another.

A fly finds it is stuck fast.

Why buy flypaper?
Instead of using flypaper,
people in countries such as
Portugal sometimes hang
up bunches of sundew
plants to catch flies.

As it struggles, more hairs bend toward it. Their sticky tips clamp the wiggling creature tightly. The more the insect struggles, the tighter the leaf grips. Eventually, the insect's body is crushed and it dies a sticky death.

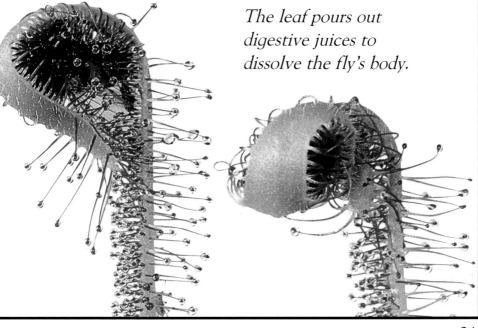

*The leaf pours out
digestive juices to
dissolve the fly's body.*

Deadly weeds

Carnivorous plants are no danger to humans, but some other plants are. If you took a walk in this North American woodland, would you spot the plants you should avoid?

Some plants make mild poisons to stop animals from eating them.

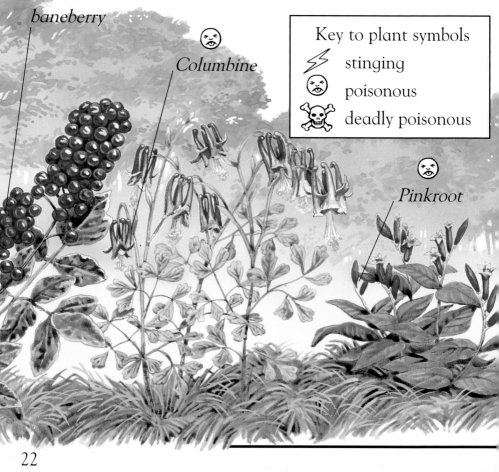

Red baneberry

Columbine

Pinkroot

Key to plant symbols

stinging

poisonous

deadly poisonous

If you touched or ate one, it would sting you or make you sick. Some plants even make poisons that can kill.

So never touch or bite a strange plant. It might bite back!

Yew

Canadian woodnettle

Water hemlock

Poison Ivy

Stinging plants use chemical weapons to keep animals from eating them.

Poison ivy is a stinging plant that grows all over North America. The plant contains a sticky oil. If you brush against the plant, the oil that oozes out from bruised leaves or stems can spread onto your skin.

Some people feel a sting immediately. Others feel nothing at first, but hours later, their skin starts to blister and itch  unbearably. In a few days, the blisters turn into oozing, crusted sores.

Fruit and nuts

Poison ivy has some delicious relatives. Cashew nuts and mango fruit grow on plants of the same family.

The glossy, pointed leaf of a poison ivy plant ___

You can develop these sores without ever touching a poison ivy plant. Its oil can be spread by pets, garden tools, sports equipment – in fact, anything that touches a bruised or broken plant.

Some stinging plants have weak chemicals, but they can still pack a painful punch. To do this they need to get their poisons right through the skin.

The stinging nettle does this with millions of tiny, hollow spikes. If you touch a stinging nettle leaf, the spikes will prick your skin. The tips of the spikes break off and release acid from the plant. The acid flows through the hollow spikes and into your skin.

The tiny, glass-like tip snaps off when the spike is touched.

The spike is filled with chemicals from base to tip.

Once the tip has broken off, the remaining point is sharp enough to pierce skin.

The acid causes a throbbing, painful, hot white rash. Fortunately, this usually goes away after an hour or two, although some people suffer for up to 24 hours.

Dock to the rescue
The dock plant, which often grows near nettles, can ease the pain of a nettle rash if its leaves are crushed and pressed onto the sting.

The base tightens and squeezes poison along the spike.

Close-up view of two nettle spikes

Nettles are not very harmful to humans, but they have a highly dangerous relative – the stinger tree of Australia. Its name alone should warn you of danger.

Stinger tree leaves are nasty weapons. They are covered in hollow hairs with very sharp tips. The hairs work like the needle of a doctor's syringe. If you touch a leaf, the hair tips break off and the hairs inject poison into your skin.

If you brush your arm against a stinger tree, it will give you a sting you will never forget. Your arm will throb painfully all day. It will still tingle two weeks later.

But if you happened to get stung all over by stinger tree leaves, the pain would be so bad you would not be able to walk or get up. You could even receive enough poison to kill you.

Many dangerous plants have no sting. Some are even quite beautiful. You would never guess from its pretty blue flowers that monkshood contains a powerful poison. Its name is aconitine (ack-oh-NIGH-teen) and even tiny amounts of it can kill.

In Italy, hundreds of years ago, murderers gave their enemies gloves dusted with aconitine powder. The poison entered the victims' bodies through cuts or scratches on their fingers.

Wolf killer
Another name for the monkshood plant is wolf's bane. It got this name because its roots were once used to poison wolves.

A cut-up monkshood flower

The roots, leaves, stems, and even the flowers of the monkshood are poisonous.

Like the monkshood, the bright red seeds of the prayer bean plant look harmless. People in India used the seeds to make necklaces and rosaries.

But wearing a prayer bean necklace is a bad idea. Each little seed contains enough poison to kill a grown-up. If the tough outer casing of the seed is broken or cracked, the poison inside escapes. It can enter the body through a scratch or cut.

Weighing them up

Because prayer bean seeds are all nearly exactly the same weight and size, they were once used as weights to weigh gold and diamonds.

Prayer bean plant

Malaysian people frightened the first European visitors to their land with tales of the deadly upas tree. They called it the tree of poisons. They said that the tree killed birds flying over it, and that anyone who slept in its shade would never wake up.

Seven hundred years later we know that these stories are untrue. Birds perch unharmed in the tree's branches, and sleeping under the tree is perfectly safe.

However, the sap of the tree contains a deadly poison. A scratch from the bark causes a painful rash. Poison taken from the sap can stop the heart from beating in just a few minutes. Local people once executed prisoners by tying them to the tree, or by stabbing them with a stick dipped in the poison.

Engraving from an old book of poisons showing the deadly upas tree

In the depths of the Amazon rainforest grow thousands of kinds of bushes, vines, and trees. Here, the native people found the ingredients to make one of the world's most powerful natural poisons: curare.

The native people used the poison to hunt animals. To get the poison, they soaked the bark and roots of certain plants in water, then boiled the water to make a paste. They smeared the paste on small darts and shot the darts from long bamboo blowpipes.

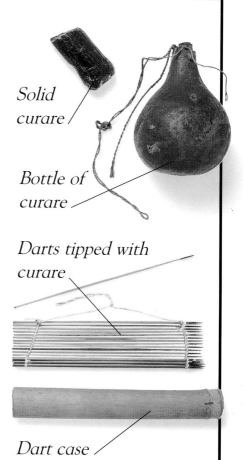

Solid curare

Bottle of curare

Darts tipped with curare

Dart case

The hunters shot monkeys to test the poison. If the monkey fell quickly from a tree, the poison was "one-tree" poison – the strongest. If the monkey swung to another tree before falling, the poison was "two-tree" poison. "Three-tree" poison was rejected as too weak.

Nature's daggers

Many plants protect themselves with thorns, spikes and spines instead of poison. These prickly, pesky plants sprout almost everywhere.

Bramble

In the deserts of America grow the spiniest of all plants – the cactus family. Cacti (plural for "cactus") have spines instead of leaves. These sharp spines keep thirsty animals from munching the cactus's juicy stem. The spines also help the cactus to get water. Mist and dew collect on the spines and drip or trickle down to water the cactus's roots.

Cactus plants can get very tall. The biggest is the Saguaro cactus. In 150 years it can grow as big as a five-storey building.

Right: Saguaro cactus

The spines of the Mexican "hedgehog" cactus are like daggers. The Aztecs of ancient Mexico had a grisly use for  this plant. If one of their gods demanded a gift of human blood, they stretched prisoners across the cactus. The spines pierced the prisoners' bodies.

Aztec warriors capture victims for sacrifice on a cactus

Going fishing?
In the past, people have used the strong, hooked spines of the "barrel" cactus as fishing hooks.

Cactus spines are bad enough, but the tufts of stiff, fine hair that grow on some cacti can also cause terrible pain. Each hair has a hook on the end. Once stuck in your flesh, the hairs are almost impossible to remove.

The fluffy stems look like rabbits' ears.

Many people have innocent-looking "bunny ears" cacti in their homes. They are part of the prickly pear family and have hundreds of hairs on each of their pads (flattened stems).

Poinsettia

Gardeners love spurge plants. They are fleshy, bushy shrubs with colorful leaves and flowers. The popular poinsettia plant is a member of the spurge family.

Many wild spurges are spiny as well as colorful. The sharpest, spikiest spurge of all is the candelabra tree.

The candelabra tree gets its name from its unusual shape. If it were smaller it would look like a candelabra, or candle stand. However, candelabra trees are not small. They are huge.

Look out!

Candelabra tree stems contain milky sap that can burn your skin and even cause blindness if it gets in your eyes.

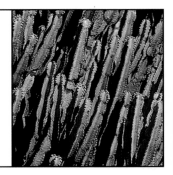

A candelabra tree growing on the African plains

A spiky candelabra stem

In South Africa, where they grow wild, candelabra trees may reach the height of a house.

In some areas, the parents of twins plant a pair of the trees in front of their home to mark the birth. They believe that the trees ward off evil spirits and protect the children. Nobody dares cut down these trees, even when the home is gone and the twins are long dead.

Taming the plants

Plants that bite back are not bad plants. They are just plants that have smart ways of surviving in a tough world. And while we humans may curse their prickles and stings, we have also learned how useful they can be.

Cattle herders in some parts of Africa build thorny fences to keep their animals safe. In Mexico, burglar-proof hedges of prickly pear cacti protect some homes.

Even stinging plants have had their uses to humans.

In chilly weather, Roman soldiers warmed their legs by beating them with nettle plants.

Women once used plants instead of makeup. They rubbed their cheeks with the woolly leaves of mullein plants. Mullein leaves are covered in soft, fine hairs. These hairs irritated the women's skin and gave their cheeks a bright, rosy glow.

Mullein plant

But what use is a **poison**ous plant? The answer may surprise you. Plant poisons that kill in large doses can heal in smaller amounts.

Doctors once used aconitine, from the deadly monkshood plant, to help calm patients' nerves.

You could die from heart failure if you ate just four leaves from the foxglove plant. But foxglove poison is now used to treat some heart disorders.

Foxglove

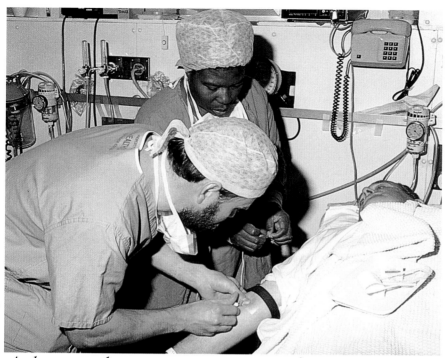
A doctor and nurse prepare a patient for surgery.

Yew

Doctors once used curare to relax patients' muscles before surgery.

And today, scientists are extracting anti-cancer drugs from the poisonous yew tree.

Who knows what uses will be found for deadly plants in the future?

Glossary

Absorb
To soak up or take in something.

Acid
A burning chemical.

Aconitine
A deadly poison found in the monkshood plant.

Amazon rainforest
A very wet forest by the Amazon River in South America.

Bait
Something that encourages prey to come closer to a trap.

Bane
An old-fashioned word for poison.

Bog, marsh, swamp
Different kinds of wet, spongy land.

Cactus
A family of North American plants with fleshy stems used to store water.

Carnivorous plant
A plant that gets extra minerals from the dead bodies of animals.

Curare
An arrow poison made from a mixture of plants.

Desert
Land where little or no rain falls.

Digestive juices
Liquid filled with chemicals that help to break down food so that it can be absorbed by a plant or animal.

Fry
Baby fish.

Glands
Structures inside a plant or animal that produce chemicals such as digestive juices.

Insect
A six-legged animal with no backbone. Its body is divided into three parts.

Larva
A young animal that is completely different from an adult animal of the same kind. For example, a caterpillar is the larva of a butterfly.

Microscope
An instrument for looking at tiny things. It has lenses that make things look bigger.

Minerals
Inorganic (neither plant nor animal) substances that all living things need in order to grow.

Nectar
A liquid made by flowering plants.

Poison
A substance that kills or damages living things.

Prey
Animals that are caught and eaten by plants or other animals.

Root
The part of a plant that takes in water and minerals.

Trigger hairs
Sensitive hairs that grow on plants near their traps. If touched, the hairs send a message to the plant to make it shut its trap.